FUN WITH PEANUTS®

FUN WITH

Selected Cartoons from
GOOD OL' CHARLIE BROWN
(Volume 1)

PEANUTS®

by Charles M. Schulz

A FAWCETT CREST BOOK
FAWCETT PUBLICATIONS, INC., GREENWICH, CONN.
MEMBER OF AMERICAN BOOK PUBLISHERS COUNCIL, INC.

FUN WITH PEANUTS

This book, prepared especially for Fawcett Publications, Inc., comprises the first half of GOOD OL' CHARLIE BROWN, and is reprinted by arrangement with Holt, Rinehart and Winston, Inc.

Eleventh Fawcett Crest printing, September 1967

Published by Fawcett World Library,
67 West 44th Street, New York, New York 10036.
Printed in the United States of America.

HI, CHARLIE BROWN..
HI, GIRLS..
GOOD OL' CHARLIE BROWN
GEE..I HEARD ONE OF THEM SAY, "GOOD OL' CHARLIE BROWN.." MAYBE THOSE GIRLS DON'T THINK I'M SO BAD AFTER ALL...
GOOD OL' WISHY-WASHY CHARLIE BROWN!
SCHULZ

?
AARGH
!
HERE IT IS, LINUS! ALL FLUFFY AN' CLEAN!
SIGH
LINUS REALLY SUFFERS ON THE DAY HIS BLANKET IS BEING WASHED..
SCHULZ

I GET SO TIRED OF BEING JUST A DOG!

WHAT A MISERABLE LIFE!

I'M TIRED OF **BEING** A DOG AND I'M TIRED OF **ASSOCIATING** WITH DOGS!

IF I WERE A HUMAN BEING I WOULDN'T EVEN **OWN** A DOG!
SCHULZ

YOU FASCINATE ME!
SCHULZ

ISN'T THAT 'PIG-PEN' A MESS?

LOOK AT HIS CLOTHES..AND HIS HAIR...AND THAT DIRTY FACE..

YOU KNOW WHAT HE LOOKS LIKE?
WHAT?

A HUMAN SOIL-BANK!
SCHULZ

HERE Y'ARE, SNOOPY...A NICE DISH OF WATER
GOOD GRIEF! WHAT A FUSSY DOG!
WHAT'S THE MATTER?
NO ICE CUBES!
SCHULZ

WHAT A MESS!
BROKEN TOYS ALL OVER THE YARD...
DON'T YOU EVER PICK THEM UP, CHARLIE BROWN?
NOPE..
I THINK THINGS LIKE THAT SHOULD BE LEFT TO RETURN TO THE SOIL FROM WHENCE THEY CAME...
VAN
SCHULZ

I GUESS I HAVE TO LEAVE..I HEAR MY MOTHER CALLING...

I DIDN'T HEAR ANYONE CALLING, CHARLIE BROWN..
YOU SHOULD BE GLAD THAT YOU DIDN'T...

HER MOTHER USES A WHISTLE THAT ONLY FUSS-BUDGETS CAN HEAR
SCHULZ

LET ME POUND IN THE STAKES, CHARLIE BROWN..

OKAY...WHILE YOU'RE DOING THAT, I'LL SET UP ALL THE WICKETS...

WHAPETY
WHAPETY
WHAPETY
WHAPETY
WHAPETY
WHAP

OH, GOOD GRIEF!
Schulz

CHARLIE BROWN, I'VE TOLD YOU A MILLION TIMES...
I DON'T WANT TO BE YOUR FRIEND! I JUST DON'T WANT TO!
rats
COULDN'T YOU AT LEAST BE A 'FAIR-WEATHER FRIEND'?
SCHULZ

LOOK, SCHROEDER.. THE CATCHER IS SUPPOSED TO BE THE BACKBONE OF THE TEAM..
HOW ABOUT SHOWING A LITTLE SPIRIT? CAN'T YOU YELL A LITTLE OR WHISTLE?!
"NOCTURNE IN E FLAT MAJOR" BY CHOPIN
GOOD GRIEF!

CHARLIE BROWN, I CAN'T GET OUT FAR ENOUGH IN LEFT FIELD..
THAT HOUSE IS RIGHT IN THE WAY!
I KNOW IT IS.. YOU'LL JUST HAVE TO DO THE BEST YOU CAN...
SCHULZ

I NEVER REALIZED THE TROUBLES THAT A BASEBALL MANAGER HAS.. EVERYBODY COMES TO HIM WITH THEIR PROBLEMS...

HEY, MANAGER... TIE MY SHOE!
SURE

!

GET OUT OF HERE!!
SCHULZ

HEY, AREN'T WE SHORT ONE MAN? WHERE'S 'PIG-PEN'?

HE'S RIGHT WHERE YOU PUT HIM...AT SECOND BASE..

OH, YES, SO HE IS..

HE'S HARD TO SEE BECAUSE HE BLENDS IN WITH THE DIRT ON THE INFIELD!
SCHULZ

HEY, MANAGER! I'VE GOT GOOD NEWS FOR YOU..

YESTERDAY I GOT HIT ON THE HEAD WITH FOUR BALLS AND CAUGHT THREE...

TODAY I GOT HIT ON THE HEAD WITH ONLY THREE BALLS AND CAUGHT FOUR!

IF THAT ISN'T IMPROVEMENT, I DON'T KNOW WHAT IS!!
SCHULZ

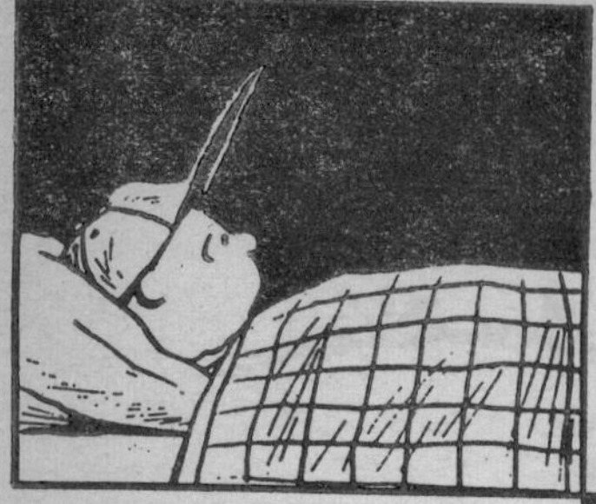
MONDAY IS OUR FIRST GAME, AND I'M SCARED TO DEATH..

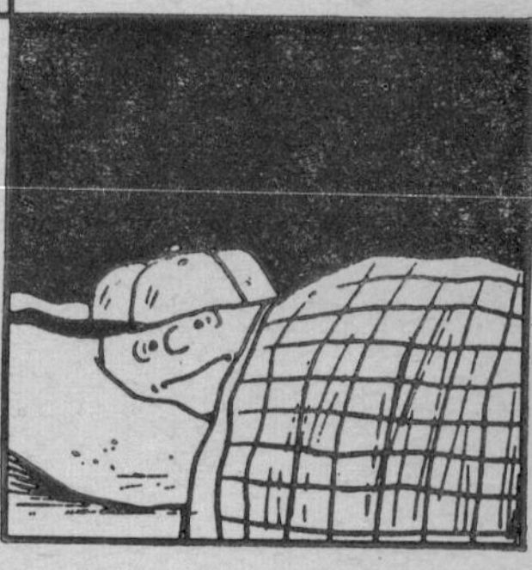
WHAT A TEAM I'VE GOT... FIVE BOYS, THREE GIRLS AND A DOG! GOOD GRIEF!!
I DON'T KNOW WHY I EVER TRIED TO BE A MANAGER..I MUST BE OUT OF MY MIND!

I WONDER IF CASEY STENGEL IS ASLEEP?
SCHULZ

NOBODY LIKES ME...NOBODY!
HAVE YOU EVER STOPPED TO TRY TO FIGURE OUT WHY NOBODY LIKES YOU, CHARLIE BROWN?
OF COURSE, I HAVE...AND I FOUND OUT WHY, TOO...
I'M UNPOPULAR!
SCHULZ

LISTEN TO THIS, LINUS...
ONE HUNDRED AND FORTY-FIVE YEARS AGO TODAY THE FIRST STEAMSHIP CROSSED THE ATLANTIC..
THAT WAS IN 1819!
1819?
WERE THERE PEOPLE THEN?!
SCHULZ

DOES RUBBING A BALLOON BOTHER YOU, VIOLET?

NO, NOT IN THE LEAST
IT DOESN'T BOTHER ME, EITHER
SQUEAK
SQUEAK

THEY SAY IT DOES BOTHER SOME PEOPLE, THOUGH..
YES, I'VE HEARD THAT IT DOES
SKWEEK
SKWEEK

I WONDER WHAT SORT OF PEOPLE IT BOTHERS..
I DON'T KNOW.. IT SURE DOESN'T BOTHER ME..
SQUEAK
SQUEAK
SCHULZ

I GIVE UP...THERE'S NO USE TRYING..
STORIES

NO MATTER HOW HARD I TRY, I CAN'T READ BETWEEN THE LINES!
STORIES
SCHULZ

YOU DIDN'T KNOW I WAS A REAL MUSIC LOVER, DID YOU, SCHROEDER?

OH, YES. I HAVE A GREAT LOVE FOR GOOD MUSIC...

MY FAVORITE PIECE IS BACH'S TOCCATA AND FUGUE IN ASIA MINOR..

SOMEHOW, I DON'T THINK I IMPRESSED HIM...
SCHULZ

?
?
CLICK
CLICK
CLICK
CLICK
CLICK
CLICK

?
CLICK
CLICK
CLICK
CLICK
CLICK

CLICK CLICK
CLICK CLICK
CLICK

TOENAILS!
SCHULZ

SIGH
NOBODY'S HAPPY WHERE THEY ARE...
SCHULZ

WELL, HI!
SCHULZ

KLUNK!
KLUNK?!
SCHULZ

I JUST DON'T KNOW...

I'VE HEARD A LOT OF ARGUMENTS ON BOTH SIDES..

YOU'RE IN THE FIRST GRADE, PATTY...MAYBE YOU CAN TELL US...

JUST HOW IMPORTANT IS IT TO HAVE A GOOD EDUCATION?
SCHULZ

SCHULZ

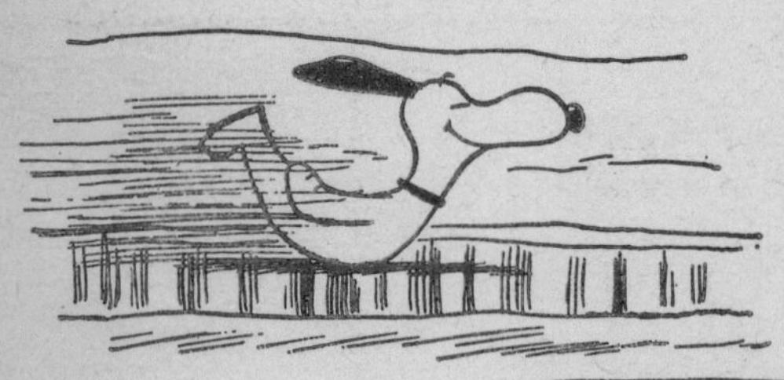

GOOD GRIEF! I THINK I FROZE MY STOMACH!
SCHULZ

PEOPLE SHOULD BE MORE KIND TO EACH OTHER
EVERYONE SHOULD TRY TO BE GENTLE AND CONSIDERATE
THAT'S TRUE..
!
!
GET OUT OF HERE! CAN'T YOU SEE WE'RE TALKING?
SCHULZ

BOY, WHAT A TOUCH! SNOOPY'S THE ONLY DOG IN THE WORLD WHO CAN RETRIEVE A SOAP-BUBBLE!
SCHULZ

KIND OF CHILLY OUT TODAY, EH, CHARLIE BROWN?
IT'S MORE THAN JUST CHILLY.. IT'S COLD OUTSIDE...
IN FACT, IT'S MORE THAN JUST **COLD**...
IT'S **MITTEN** COLD!!
SCHULZ

SCHROEDER, WHAT IF SOMEDAY YOU MADE A LOT OF MONEY PLAYING THE PIANO, AND...

HOW MANY TIMES DO I HAVE TO TELL YOU THAT I DON'T PLAY THE PIANO FOR MONEY?!!!

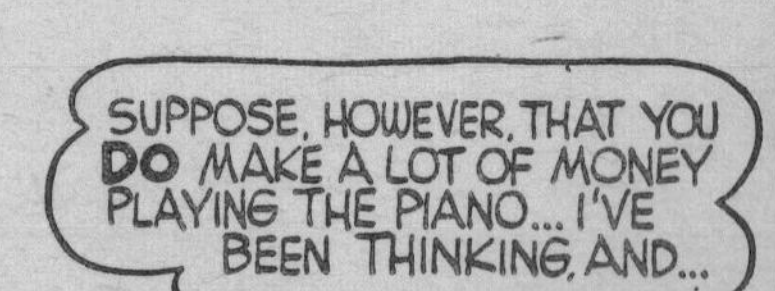

SUPPOSE, HOWEVER, THAT YOU DO MAKE A LOT OF MONEY PLAYING THE PIANO... I'VE BEEN THINKING, AND...
GOOD GRIEF!
SCHULZ

"PIG-PEN," WHY ARE YOU ALWAYS SO DIRTY?
WHEN IN THE WORLD ARE YOU GOING TO CLEAN UP?
I HAVE AFFIXED TO ME THE DIRT AND DUST OF COUNTLESS AGES..
WHO AM I TO DISTURB HISTORY?
SCHULZ

STRIKE THREE!

YOU'RE OUT LINUS!
YOU'RE OUT!

!
SIGH
SCHULZ

CLANK
CLANK
CLANK
STUPID ROLLER SKATES!
AND YOU CAN STAY IN THERE, AN' **ROT** FOR ALL **I** CARE!
SCHULZ

?
SCHULZ

HELP!
SCHULZ

WELL, THERE GOES THE OLD BALL GAME!

MY DADDY SAYS WE NEED RAIN... HE SAYS OUR LAWN IS JUST ABOUT DRIED OUT...

HE SAYS OUR GARDEN NEEDS RAIN, AND OUR NEW HEDGE NEEDS RAIN, AND HE SAYS...

OH, SHUT UP!!

HOW'S KINDERGARTEN, LUCY?

GOOD ENOUGH, I GUESS CONSIDERING IT REALLY ISN'T WHAT I HAD WANTED..

OH? HAD YOU WANTED TO GO SOMEPLACE ELSE?
SURE..

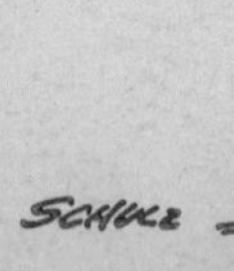
MILITARY SCHOOL!
SCHULZ

HA HA HA HA HA..
GO AHEAD AND LAUGH, CHARLIE BROWN! SOMEDAY I'LL SHOW YOU!!
?
IT'S NOT NICE TO LAUGH AT A PERSON'S AMBITIONS!!! BUT, BY GOLLY, I'LL SHOW HIM!
SOMEDAY I'LL BE A 'WHITE-COLLAR WORKER'!
SCHULZ

SO THERE, TOO!
OOooo! I SHOULD HAVE TOLD HER OFF!! OOOO, HOW I SHOULD HAVE TOLD HER OFF!
I KNEW I WAS RIGHT, TOO! I JUST KNEW IT!!
YET, I WASN'T QUITE SURE..
SCHULZ

I FELL OFF A SWING THIS MORNING, AND BUMPED MY HEAD...
YESTERDAY I SCRAPED BOTH OF MY KNEES ROLLER-SKATING...
AND THE DAY BEFORE I FELL DOWN THE STEPS PLAYING 'TAG'.....

IT LOOKS LIKE IT'S GOING TO BE A LONG SUMMER..
SCHULZ

'NATIONAL DOG WEEK'..

'IT IS, INDEED, THE HAPPY AND HARMONIOUS FAMILY WHO SHARES A DOG'S WONDERFUL QUALITIES OF LOVE, LOYALTY, WATCHFULNESS & COURAGE

..WHICH HE GIVES WITH NO THOUGHT OF REWARD..'
UUUUU

BOY, I'D BLUSH, TOO, IF I WERE YOU!
SCHULZ

IF YOU REALLY LIKED ME, CHARLIE BROWN, YOU'D CARVE OUR INITIALS IN A TREE...
ALL RIGHT...I'LL JUST DO THAT..
YOU'RE SO ROMANTIC, CHARLIE BROWN!
YEARS FROM NOW PEOPLE WILL SEE OUR INITIALS, AND..
SCHULZ

HERE COMES SHERMY... ASK HIM....

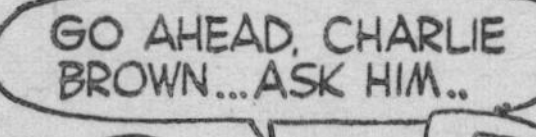
GO AHEAD, CHARLIE BROWN...ASK HIM..

YOU ASK HIM..
NO, YOU ASK HIM..

WHATEVER HAPPENED TO DAVY CROCKETT?
SCHULZ

TWANG!

RATS!

WHOP

WHAT ARE YOU TRYIN' TO DO, KILL SOMEBODY?
SCHULZ

I'LL SHOOT THE ARROW, SNOOPY, AND YOU CHASE IT....OKAY?
CLOMP!

SCHULZ

SNOOPY AND I ARE PLAYING 'THE LION AND THE HUNTER'..
I THINK HE'S TRYING TO DRAW MY FIRE..
SCHULZ

TWANG!
GOOD GRIEF!
CHASING THAT STUPID ARROW IS GOING TO DRIVE ME CRAZY!
THUMP!
SCHULZ

SOMETIMES THAT CHARLIE BROWN IS PRETTY CLEVER..
THREE BIG BOYS FROM THE SECOND GRADE WERE CHASING HIM TODAY...
HE RAN AND RAN AND RAN, BUT THEY KEPT GETTING CLOSER AND CLOSER AND CLOSER...
SUDDENLY HE ORGANIZED A DISCUSSION GROUP!
SCHULZ

I'M TRYING TO LEARN TO PLAY ALL OF THE BEETHOVEN SONATAS..

GEE...IF YOU DO LEARN TO PLAY THEM ALL, WHAT WILL YOU WIN?
I WON'T WIN ANYTHING!
YOU WON'T?

WHAT'S THE SENSE IN DOING SOMETHING IF YOU DON'T WIN A PRIZE?
SCHULZ

WHEN AUTUMN IS OVER, LINUS, WINTER COMES

AND WHEN WINTER COMES, WE CAN THROW SNOWBALLS AND MAKE SNOWMEN! WON'T THAT BE FUN?

BOY! I'LL SAY!

I WONDER WHAT 'SNOW' IS?
SCHULZ

C'MON, AND SEE THE SNOWMAN 'PIG-PEN' MADE
SAY, I'LL BET PLAYING AROUND IN THE SNOW KEPT HIM CLEAN, DIDN'T IT?
ON THE CONTRARY...

THE WORLD'S DIRTIEST SNOWMAN!
SCHULZ

YOU'LL NEVER BE GOOD AT ANYTHING, CHARLIE BROWN!
YOU'LL ALWAYS BE MEDIOCRE! DO YOU HEAR ME? JUST PLAIN MEDIOCRE!
I DON'T CARE...WHY SHOULD I CARE?
JUST SO I'M ABOVE AVERAGE!
SCHULZ

OLEE
OLEE
OLSEN
FREE-O!

OLEE
OLEE
OLSEN
FREE-O

IN CASE YOU DON'T KNOW IT, THE PHRASE IS, "ALLY, ALLY OUT ARE IN FREE!"

I'VE NEVER BEEN SO EMBARRASSED IN ALL MY LIFE...
SCHULZ

SAY, THIS IS A PRETTY GOOD BALL, CHARLIE BROWN...

I'LL HAVE YOU KNOW THIS IS AN 'OFFICIAL' BALL!

'OFFICIAL'! GEE...
YES, SIR..

THIS BALL HAS BEEN TAPED AND RE-TAPED ACCORDING TO OFFICIAL NEIGHBORHOOD-LEAGUE-STANDARDS!
SCHULZ

EXCUSE ME..I THINK SOMEBODY'S HUNGRY...
SCHULZ

MOMMY CALLED THE DOCTOR FOR YOU, LINUS..
HE'LL LOOK AT YOU, AND FIND OUT WHY YOU DON'T FEEL WELL..
WILL HE COME IN A CAR OR A TRUCK?
A CAR, I THINK..
THEN I GUESS I MUST NOT BE VERY SICK..
SCHULZ

WHAT DID THE DOCTOR DO TO YOU, LINUS?
HE TRIED TO PUT A STICK IN MY MOUTH..
BUT I WOULDN'T LET HIM DO IT...
I TOLD HIM I DIDN'T WANT THAT STICK IN MY MOUTH AFTER SOMEBODY ELSE HAD EATEN ALL THE ICE-CREAM OFF OF IT!
SCHULZ

?
SAY, I JUST SAW LINUS RUN BY...
OH?
I THOUGHT HE WAS SICK IN BED..
HE WAS...BUT HE'S NOT LIKE US, CHARLIE BROWN...
WHEN YOU'RE YOUNG YOU KNOW, YOU RECOVER FAST!
SCHULZ

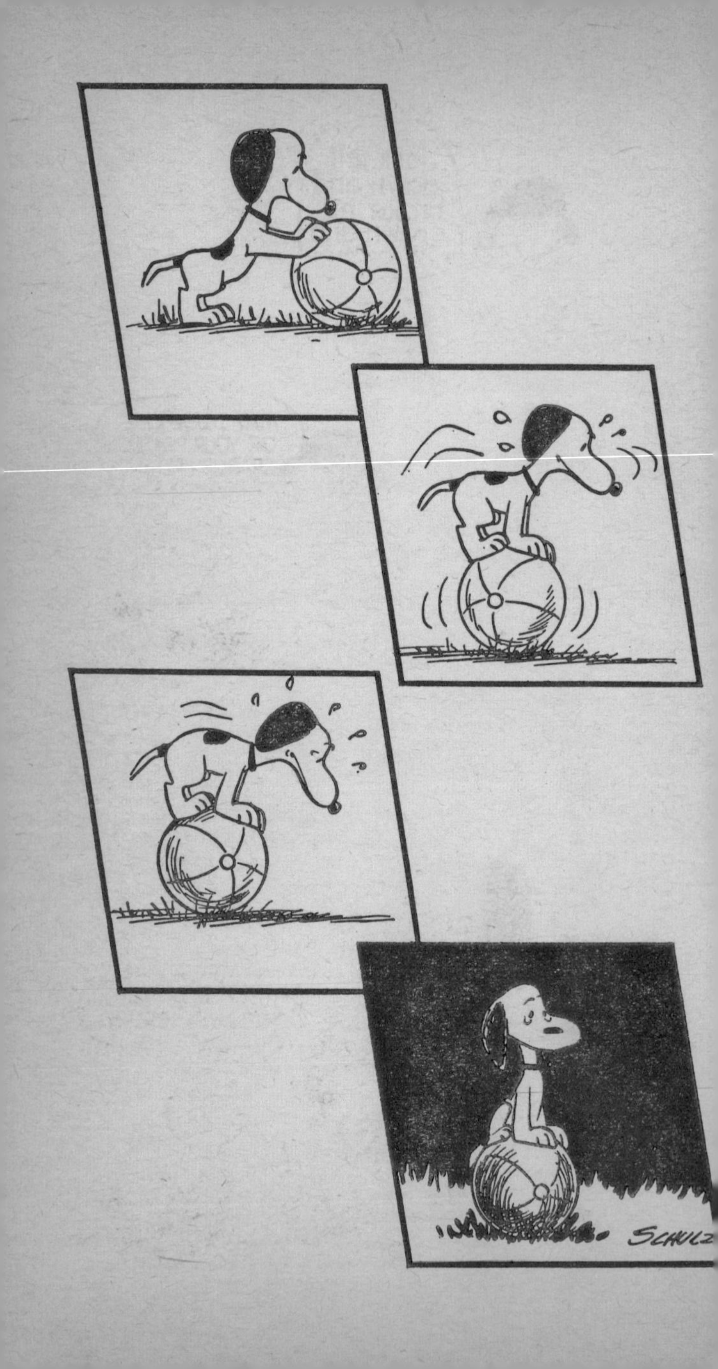
SCHULZ

"Jack fell down, and broke his crown, and Jill came tumbling after."

MAY I USE ONE OF YOUR PENCILS, CHARLIE BROWN?

THANK YOU..

I ALWAYS LIKE TO UNDERLINE PARTICULARLY SIGNIFICANT PASSAGES..
SCHULZ

THIS PROGRAM WAS SHOWN IN COMPATIBLE COLOR..
WHAT OTHER KIND OF COLOR IS THERE?
WELL THERE'S INCOMPATIBLE COLOR...
WHAT'S THAT?
THAT'S WHEN YOU HAVE COLOR T.V., BUT YOU WON'T LET CHARLIE BROWN COME OVER AND WATCH IT!
SCHULZ

I'M INDEPENDENT!
I CAN STAND ON MY OWN...

TWO FEET!
SCHULZ

BELIEVE IN ME!
BELIEVE IN ME!
BELIEVE IN ME!
I JUST CAN'T GET PEOPLE TO BELIEVE IN ME..
SCHULZ

CHARLIE BROWN, DID YOU KNOW THAT TWELVE-THOUSAND HOURS OF YOUR LIFE WILL BE SPENT IN SCHOOL?

REALLY? WHY, THAT'S INCREDIBLE!

IT'S FANTASTIC...IT'S UNBELIEVABLE...

IT'S ALSO ENOUGH TO MAKE YOU SICK...
SCHULZ

IN THE OLD DAYS PEOPLE THOUGHT THE WORLD WAS FLAT..
REALLY?

THEY THOUGHT THAT IF YOU SAILED TOO FAR, YOU'D FALL OVER THE EDGE, AND BE SWALLOWED BY MONSTERS
HONESTLY?

THAT WAS KIND OF STUPID, WASN'T IT?

WHAT DO WE THINK NOWADAYS?
SCHULZ

LUCY SURE HAS BEAUTIFUL EYES, HASN'T SHE?

SOMETIMES, THOUGH, THEY SEEM A LITTLE OUT OF FOCUS..

IT FIGURES...

SOMETIMES LUCY HERSELF SEEMS A LITTLE OUT OF FOCUS!
SCHULZ

JUST LOOK AT THAT 'PIG-PEN'..
?
ISN'T HE AWFUL?
TERRIBLE... JUST TERRIBLE!
A REAL 'GOOD-FOR-NOTHING'..
I'LL SAY... A COMPLETE FLOP!
I'M WELL-READ!
SCHULZ

THE TEACHER SAID I DID REAL WELL TODAY..

SHE SAID I WAS THE BEST PUPIL IN HER WHOLE CLASS!

WELL! THAT SHOULD MAKE YOU HAPPY, CHARLIE BROWN..

UH, HUH...IT'S ALWAYS THRILLING TO BE RECOGNIZED IN ONE'S OWN LIFETIME!
SCHULZ

MOM! I'M COMING IN NOW...

WHY DON'T YOU STAY OUTSIDE, AND PLAY?
WELL...

THERE WAS THIS CATERPILLAR ON THE SIDEWALK... AND HE WAS CRAWLING RIGHT AT ME...

SO I FIGURED I MIGHT AS WELL COME IN, AN' WATCH T.V.
SCHULZ

LISTEN TO THIS, SCHROEDER..

"A NEW BEETHOVEN HALL IS BEING BUILT ON THE BANKS OF THE RHINE RIVER.."

"THE MODERN STONE STRUCTURE WILL COST OVER A MILLION DOLLARS"

SPARE NO EXPENSE!!!!!
SCHULZ

LUCY, I'M TAKING UP A COLLECTION FOR THE NEW BEETHOVEN MEMORIAL HALL.
YOU WOULDN'T BY ANY CHANCE WANT TO CONTRIBUTE A LITTLE SOMETHING, WOULD YOU?

SURE, I'D BE GLAD TO! HERE'S TEN THOUSAND DOLLARS!!
AH, HA HA HA HO HO HO
SCHULZ

HOW MUCH IS THIS BEETHOVEN BUILDING GOING TO COST?
SIX MILLION DEUTSCHEMARKS
HOW MUCH IS THAT IN OUR MONEY?
ONE MILLION, FOUR HUNDRED AND TWENTY-EIGHT THOUSAND DOLLARS
GOOD GRIEF! THEY'LL NEVER MAKE IT WITHOUT A G.I. LOAN!
SCHULZ

VIOLET, I'M TAKING UP A COLLECTION..
IT'S FOR A MEMORIAL HALL FOR THE GREATEST COMPOSER WHO EVER LIVED..
YOU'RE WASTING YOUR TIME, SCHROEDER...
THEY'VE ALREADY BUILT A MEMORIAL TO STEPHEN FOSTER!
SCHULZ

SIX CENTS! I KNOCK ON EVERY DOOR IN THE NEIGHBORHOOD, AND WHAT DO I GET? SIX CENTS!

I'M SORRY, BEETHOVEN..
I DID THE BEST I COULD..

HE SMILED AT ME!
SCHULZ

I WAS JUST TRYING TO TALK WITH THAT LITTLE GIRL UP THE STREET...
BUT I COULDN'T SAY A WORD... I JUST STOOD THERE ALL EMBARRASSED AND CONFUSED
I GOT SO SELF-CONSCIOUS I DIDN'T KNOW WHAT TO DO..
SO I HIT HER !!
SCHULZ

I WISH MORE PEOPLE WOULD LIKE ME...

I WISH THAT AT LEAST A FEW PEOPLE WOULD LIKE ME...

IN FACT, I WISH THAT JUST ONE PERSON WOULD LIKE ME...

WHILE YOU'RE AT IT, WHY DON'T YOU WISH FOR A MILLION DOLLARS?!
SCHULZ

C'MON! HIT ONE OUT HERE!!!

WHAT'S THE MATTER? CAN'T YA HIT 'EM THIS FAR? ARE Y'WEAK, OR SOMETHING ?

WHAT DO Y'THINK I'M STANDIN' OUT HERE FOR, MY HEALTH? C'MON! HIT ONE! WHAT DO...

SCHULZ

HI, 'PIG-PEN'.. WHERE YA GOIN'?

AS THE DUCK IS DRAWN TO THE POND, AND AS THE RABBIT IS DRAWN TO THE BRIAR PATCH..
SO AM I DRAWN TO THE MUD PUDDLE!

Good grief!
SCHULZ

I HEARD YOUR MOTHER CALL YOU A 'FUSSBUDGET' THIS MORNING, LUCY...

I'M USED TO THAT
HOW ABOUT LINUS? IS HE A FUSSBUDGET, TOO?

OH, NO...NOT YET...

HE'S SORT OF AN 'APPRENTICE FUSSBUDGET!'
SCHULZ

"A MUSIC PUBLISHER CAME TO BEETHOVEN ONE DAY, AND OFFERED HIM FIFTY DOLLARS FOR A NEW PIECE.."

"'MY PRICE IS ONE HUNDRED DOLLARS,' SAID BEETHOVEN.."

"'FIFTY DOLLARS,' SAID THE PUBLISHER, 'AND NOT ONE CENT MORE!'"

DON'T LET HIM BLUFF YOU, BEETHOVEN!
SCHULZ

"'NO! NO! NO!' THE GIRL SAID TO BEETHOVEN."

"'I COULD NEVER MARRY SUCH A HORRIBLE MAN AS YOU!'"

SIGH

YOU'RE ALL ALIKE!!!
SCHULZ

I'M INDEPENDENT!
I STAND ON MY OWN TWO FEET! I DON'T NEED ANYBODY!
?
LUCY, WILL YOU TIE MY SHOE FOR ME?
SCHULZ

AREN'T THE STARS BEAUTIFUL CHARLIE BROWN?
UH, HUH

LET'S GO INSIDE AND WATCH TELEVISION...

I'M BEGINNING TO FEEL INSIGNIFICANT..

CAN YOU TAKE A LITTLE FRIENDLY CRITICISM, CHARLIE BROWN?

WHY, OF COURSE...I'M NOT ABOVE THAT SORT OF THING AT ALL..

A LITTLE FRIENDLY CRITICISM CAN ALWAYS BE HELPFUL TO A PERSON.. WHAT IS IT YOU WANTED TO SAY?

YOU'RE KIND OF STUPID
SCHULZ

TWENTY-TWO, TWENTY-THREE; TWENTY-FOUR, TWENTY-FIVE...
TWENTY-
SIX..
TWENTY-
SEVEN..
PEEKED? HOW COULD I HAVE PEEKED WHEN I WAS STANDING BEHIND A TREE?!
SCHULZ

SOMETIMES I WISH I WERE A SNAKE!
BOY, I'D SLITHER ALONG THE GROUND, AND SNEAK UP ON ALL SORTS OF PEOPLE...
ON SECOND THOUGHT, MAYBE THAT WOULDN'T BE SO GOOD..
IT'S KIND OF HARD ON THE STOMACH
SCHULZ

TOSS THAT PENNY IN THE AIR, AND I'LL SHOW YOU SOMETHING..
O.K.... SHOW ME SOMETHING...
BANG!
FASTEST GUN IN THE WEST!
SCHULZ

Z

?

BANG!

IT WAS THE ONLY MERCIFUL THING TO DO
SCHULZ

LINUS, YOU'VE GOT TO STOP THIS SHOOTING BUSINESS!
IT'S STUPID, AND IT'S VERY ANNOYING TO EVERYONE! DO YOU UNDERSTAND?
SURE..
GOOD...I'M GLAD THAT'S SETTLED...
BANG!
SCHULZ

LINUS, MOMMY SAYS TO STOP SHOOTING EVERYBODY..

SHE SAYS IF YOU DO IT ONCE MORE, YOU'LL GET SPANKED GOOD AND HARD

WELL... BACK TO THE OLD BLANKET..
SCHULZ

Billy and Susie are twins. They live in the city.

Here is their house. It is white. Here is their car. It is red.

In the morning Father goes to work. Mother cleans the house. The children play in the yard.

HERE'S A BOOK I THINK MAYBE YOU'LL LIKE, CHARLIE BROWN... IT GIVES A FASCINATING DESCRIPTION OF LIFE IN THE CITY!
SCHULZ

!
RATS!
IN ONE MINUTE THE RAIN HAS WASHED AWAY WHAT TOOK ME ALL DAY TO ACCOMPLISH!
SCHULZ

!

SHUDDER!

HE WAS EATING ANIMAL CRACKERS AND.. AND...AND.. SMILING!!
SCHULZ

DO YOU HAVE MUD-PIE SANDWICHES TO TAKE OUT?

YES, WE DO... WOULD YOU LIKE YOURS 'WITH' OR 'WITHOUT'?

'WITH' OR 'WITHOUT' WHAT? ONIONS?

NO... CRABGRASS!
SCHULZ

"ONE DAY SOMEONE ASKED LINCOLN HOW LONG A MAN'S LEGS SHOULD BE.."

"'JUST LONG ENOUGH TO REACH THE GROUND,' HE REPLIED."

DID LINCOLN REALLY SAY THAT?
SURE

I THOUGHT IT WAS BEETHOVEN!
SCHULZ

BOY, IF THAT DOESN'T TAKE THE CAKE!
WHAT'S THE MATTER, LUCY?
THAT GIRL IN THE NEXT BLOCK..
SHE GOT MAD JUST BECAUSE I HIT HER BROTHER...
I WOULDN'T GET MAD IF SHE HIT MY BROTHER!
SCHULZ

STOP IT! STOP IT THIS INSTANT! WITH ALL THE TROUBLE THERE IS IN THIS WORLD, YOU HAVE NO RIGHT TO BE SO HAPPY!!
SHE'S RIGHT...I'VE GOT TO START ACTING MORE SENSIBLE...

...TOMORROW!
SCHULZ

!

I THOUGHT I TOLD YOU TO STOP THAT DANCING?! YOU HAVE NO RIGHT TO BE SO HAPPY!!! NOW, STOP IT! DO YOU HEAR ME?!

SCHULZ

WHAT'S THAT DOTTED LINE ON YOUR BLANKET FOR, LINUS?
RIP!
!
HAPPINESS SHOULD BE SHARED!
SCHULZ

I'VE DECIDED TO MAKE SOME NEW YEAR'S RESOLUTIONS.
IN APRIL? YOU'RE A LITTLE LATE DON'T YOU THINK?
NOT AT ALL..
SMACK
I HAVE MY OWN FISCAL YEAR!
SCHULZ

JUST HOW WOULD YOU DESCRIBE 'PIG-PEN' VIOLET?
!
DIRTY HANDS, DIRTY FACE, DIRTY SHIRT AND DIRTY OVERALLS..
A PERFECT DESCRIPTION!
SHE FORGOT ONE THING...
AN IMMACULATELY CLEAN CONSCIENCE!
SCHULZ

HEY, LINUS, HOW DOES THAT THUMB TASTE?
HEY, LINUS, DOES THAT THUMB TASTE REAL GOOD?
HEY, LINUS, HOW DOES THAT THUMB TASTE?
DON'T SAY IT!!
?
SCHULZ

I'M HAVING A BIG PARTY, CHARLIE BROWN, BUT I'M NOT GOING TO INVITE YOU!!

RATS!
DON'T LET IT BOTHER YOU... SHE'S JUST BEING MEAN..

I CAN'T HELP IT!! RATS! RATS! RATS!

WHENEVER SHE GOES TO ALL THAT TROUBLE TO HURT ME, I SORT OF FEEL OBLIGATED TO LET IT BOTHER ME..
SCHULZ

OH, HOW I HATE TO SEE WINTER COME... SNOW AND ICE AND...

!

SLEET AND WIND AND BITTER COLD AND...
SCHULZ

ANOTHER FEW WEEKS AND ALL THE BIRDS WILL BE COMING BACK...

COMING BACK? COMING BACK FROM WHERE?
FROM THE SOUTH.. DIDN'T YOU KNOW THAT BIRDS FLY SOUTH FOR THE WINTER?

HA HA HAHAHAHA

IN ALL MY LIFE, CHARLIE BROWN, I'VE NEVER KNOWN ANYONE WITH AN IMAGINATION LIKE YOURS!
SCHULZ

I TELL YOU, LUCY, BIRDS DO FLY SOUTH DURING THE WINTER!

SURE, THEY DO, CHARLIE BROWN... AND THEY FLY WEST DURING THE SPRING AND EAST DURING THE FALL

HA! HA! HA! HA! HA!

I FEEL LIKE GOING HOME TO BED, BUT IT'S ONLY NOON...
SCHULZ

YOU NEVER SEE A CHICKEN FLYING SOUTH FOR THE WINTER, DO YOU?

HAVE YOU EVER SEEN A CHICKEN FLYING SOUTH?

CHICKENS ARE BIRDS, AREN'T THEY?

I ASKED MY TEACHER TODAY ABOUT THIS BIRD BUSINESS..
OH?

SHE SAID YOU WERE RIGHT, CHARLIE BROWN...SOME BIRDS DO FLY SOUTH DURING THE WINTER..

YOU KNOW WHAT?
WHAT?

I THINK I'LL SEE IF THEY'LL LET ME CHANGE TEACHERS..
SCHULZ

I WISH I KNEW **WHY** PEOPLE DON'T LIKE ME...I WISH I KNEW THE **REASONS**..

DO YOU HAVE A PIECE OF PAPER?
I CAN GET ONE..

ALL RIGHT...NOW DIVIDE THE PAPER INTO TEN COLUMNS...THEN PUT NUMBERS DOWN THE LEFT SIDE FROM ONE TO A HUNDRED...
!

MAYBE YOU'D BETTER CALL THIS FIRST SHEET "A," IN CASE WE RUN OUT OF ROOM, AND HAVE TO USE MORE PAPER...
SIGH
SCHULZ

'PIG-PEN,' YOU'RE AN ABSOLUTE MESS!

HERE, I WANT YOU TO LOOK AT YOURSELF IN THIS MIRROR...

NOW! AREN'T YOU ASHAMED?
ON THE CONTRARY...

I DIDN'T THINK I LOOKED THAT GOOD!
SCHULZ

HEY, CHARLIE BROWN...DO YOU WANT ME TO FEED SNOOPY BEFORE WE GO?
SURE...HIS DOG FOOD IS RIGHT THERE IN THE CUPBOARD..
DID YOU PUT IT IN HIS DISH?
OF COURSE..
?
DOG FOOD
SCHULZ
SCHULZ

YOU SHOULDN'T BE SUCKING YOUR THUMB, LINUS...
GRANDMA SAYS IT'LL MAKE YOUR TEETH CROOKED..
OH, GOOD GRIEF...
WHICH WOULD YOU RATHER SEE ME HAVE...CROOKED TEETH OR A WARPED PERSONALITY?
SCHULZ

MOST GREAT COMPOSERS WERE INSPIRED BY WOMEN.. DO I INSPIRE YOU, SCHROEDER?
YOU'D INSPIRE ME A LOT IF YOU'D JUST GO AWAY!!

I'M AFRAID YOU'RE DOOMED TO BE A FAILURE, SCHROEDER..

YOU CAN'T BE A GREAT COMPOSER AND FIGHT AGAINST INSPIRATION..
SCHULZ

A GOOD CENTERFIELDER IS THE BACKBONE OF A TEAM!

YES, SIR.. CENTERFIELD IS THE MOST IMPORTANT POSITION ON THE WHOLE TEAM..

HEY!

HOW ABOUT LETTING **ME** PLAY IN THE INFIELD FOR AWHILE?
SCHULZ

I HAVE TO GO TO THE DOCTOR THIS AFTERNOON..
IT'S TIME FOR ANOTHER SHOT.. I WONDER IF I'LL FEEL IT?
WHY? YOU'RE NOT AFRAID OF A LITTLE PAIN, ARE YOU?
I SURE AM!

PAIN HURTS!
SCHULZ

BOY, IF I WERE A SNAKE, I'D SURE SCARE A LOT OF PEOPLE I KNOW

HISS! HISS! HISS!

HISS! HISS! HISS!

SIGH
SCHULZ

I THINK BEING A SNAKE WOULD BE A GOOD DEAL..

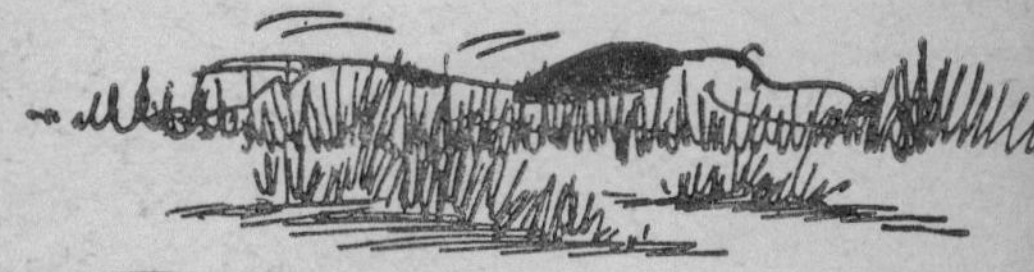
ALL YOU'D HAVE TO DO ALL DAY LONG IS CRAWL AROUND IN THE GRASS..

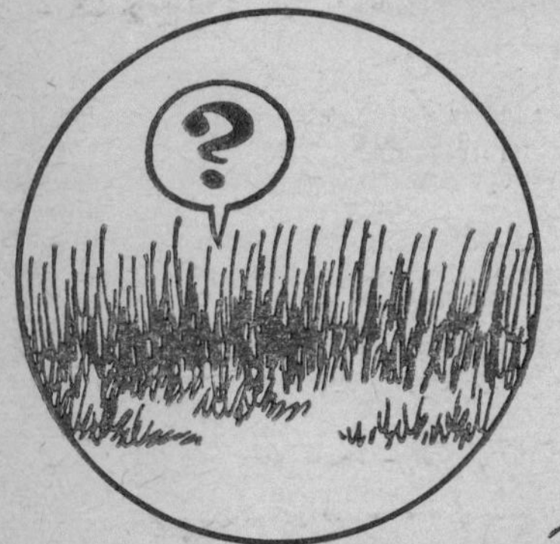
?

HOW IN THE WORLD DO THEY SEE WHERE THEY'RE GOING?

HISS! HISS! HISS!
!

SNAKE

SNAKE! SNAKE! HIT HIM WITH A CLUB! KILL HIM! KILL HIM! HIT HIM WITH A SHOVEL!!!
WHEW!
SCHULZ

BOY, IT'S HOT TODAY...
GOOD MORNING, PATTY... GOOD MORNING, CHARLIE BROWN... BEAUTIFUL DAY, ISN'T IT?
THE HEAT DOESN'T SEEM TO BE BOTHERING 'PIG-PEN' MUCH..
I THINK HE'S PROBABLY COOLED BY SEVERAL LAYERS OF CLAY!
SCHULZ

I'M GOING TO HAVE A PARTY, CHARLIE BROWN, AND I'M NOT GOING TO INVITE YOU..

NYAHH, NYAHH, NYAHH!
I DON'T MIND NOT BEING INVITED TO HER PARTY...

IT'S THOSE '**NYAHHS**' THAT GET ME!
SCHULZ

I'VE BEEN WATCHING THESE BUGS, CHARLIE BROWN...

YOU SEE, THIS ONE BUG HERE IS ABOUT TO LEAVE HOME.. HE'S BEEN SAYING GOOD-BYE TO ALL HIS FRIENDS

SUDDENLY THIS LITTLE GIRL BUG COMES RUNNING UP, AND TRIES TO PERSUADE HIM NOT TO LEAVE...

IF YOU'RE GOING TO BE A GOOD 'BUG-WATCHER,' YOU HAVE TO HAVE LOTS OF IMAGINATION!
SCHULZ